CRAFTY IDEAS WITH
MUSICAL INSTRUMENTS

Melanie Rice

Illustrated by Lynne Farmer

Photography by Chris Fairclough

HODDER AND STOUGHTON
LONDON   SYDNEY   AUCKLAND   TORONTO

**To Chris, Catherine and Alex,
for all their help.**

British Library Cataloguing in Publication Data

Rice, Melanie
    Crafty ideas with musical instruments.
    I. Title   II. Series
    745.59

    ISBN 0-340-55092-9

First published 1991

Published by Hodder and Stoughton Children's Books,
a division of Hodder and Stoughton Ltd,
Mill Road, Dunton Green, Sevenoaks, Kent TN13 2YA

Cover illustration by Lynn Breeze

Design by Sally Boothroyd

Book list compiled by Peter Bone,
Area Schools Librarian (Portsmouth),
Hampshire County Library

Printed in Belgium by Proost International Book Production

CONTENTS

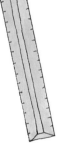

Note to parents and teachers

All the ideas in this book are easy to carry out at home or at school. Every item has been made by my own young children and then photographed for this book. Each page has clear instructions accompanied by numbered easy-to-follow illustrations.

Most of the instruments can be made from materials found around the house. However, you will need to buy plywood off-cuts from your local D.I.Y. shop and one or two other odds and ends. For some of the activities the children will need to use saws, pliers, hammers etc. Needless to say, they should be supervised by an adult at these times.

I recommend PVA adhesive for sticking wood as well as card. Poster paints with their strong bright colours are more effective on wood than watercolours.

I have tried to cover as many types of instrument as possible: strings, woodwind and percussion, but unfortunately there will be no brass section in your do-it-yourself orchestra.

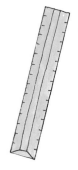

Note to children

Things to remember:

1 Read all the instructions carefully before you begin so that you know what you have to do. Use the illustrations to help you.

2 Make sure everything you need is ready before you start.

3 Use saws and other tools with great care.

4 Spread newspaper over your working surface when you are sticking or painting.

5 Clean up any mess after you have finished.

6 Put everything away tidily.

At the end of some projects I have suggested more things for you to make. Maybe you have some ideas of your own. Don't be afraid to try them out.

Melanie Rice

TUBULAR BELLS

Players in Javanese gamelan orchestras use gongs and chime bars to make ringing sounds. These bells can be part of your own gamelan orchestra.

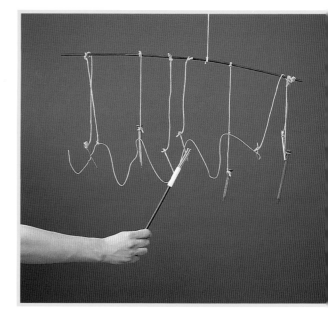

You will need:

10 nails
pliers
scissors
stick (60cm)
stick (20cm)
sticky tape
string
wire coat-hanger

1 Unwind and straighten a wire coat-hanger. Bend it into a snake shape, using pliers if necessary.

2 Tie 20cm of string to each end of the wire, then hang from the 60cm stick.

1.

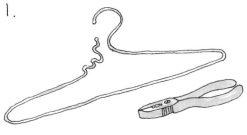

2.

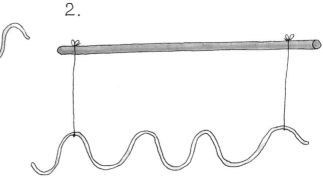

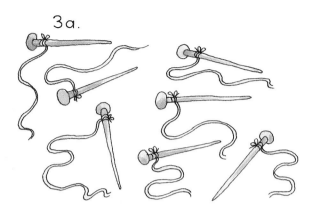

3a.

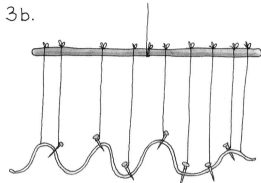

3b.

3 Tie pieces of string to seven of the nails and hang each from the stick.

4.

4 To make the beater, tape the other three nails firmly to the end of the 20cm stick.

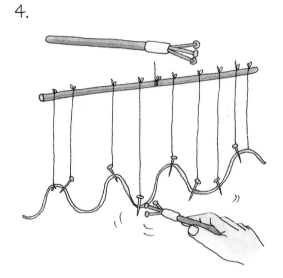

5 Hold the long stick in one hand and hit the nails with the beater so that they clang against the wire.

Bells can be made from foil, clay flower pots, coconut shells, bottle tops and many other things.

TAMBOURINE

People have danced to the sound of tambourines for thousands of years. This brightly painted tambourine jangles when you strike it with the palm of your hand.

You will need:

24 milk bottle tops
needle
paint
3 paper plates
paste
scissors
strong thread

1 Paste three paper plates together, one on top of the other.

2 Paint a bright pattern on top.

3 Cut a length of strong thread. Tie a knot at one end.

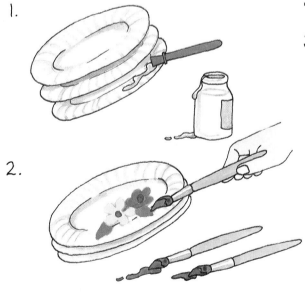

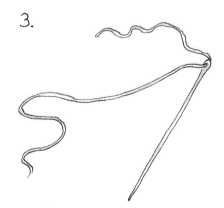

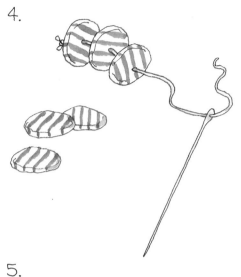

4.

4 Thread three milk bottle tops on to the cotton, then thread one end through the rim of the plates.

5 Tie the two ends of cotton together loosely so that the milk bottle tops can be shaken around.

6 Repeat 3, 4 and 5 seven more times until the circle is complete.

5.

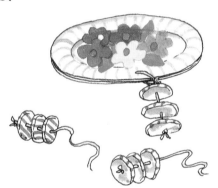

6.

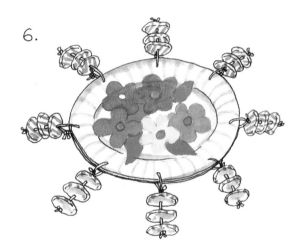

You can make a morris dancer's pole either by tying a loop of metal bottle tops to an old broom handle or by nailing some of the tops loosely to the side. Bang the stick on the ground and the bottle tops will jangle like bells.

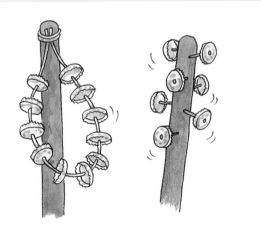

SHELL CLAPPERS

Our shell clappers make a light clicking noise like the castanets used by Spanish flamenco dancers.

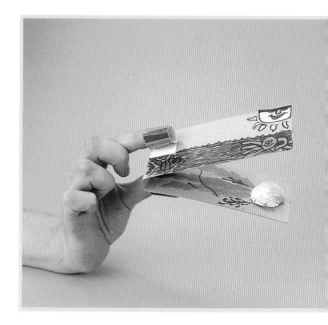

You will need:

card
paints or pens
paste
2 shells

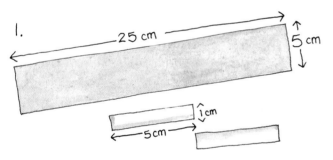

1.

2.

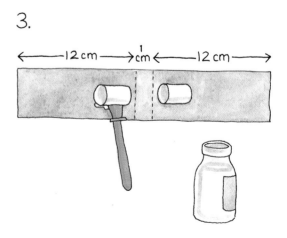

3.

1 Cut a piece of card 25cm × 5cm and two strips 5cm × 1cm.

2 Roll the strips into rings around your thumb and index finger. Paste them firmly.

3 In the middle of the card draw two dotted lines, 1cm apart. Stick on the rings, one each side of the lines as shown.

4.

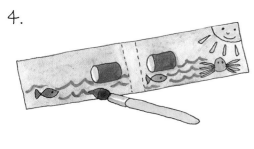

5.

6.

4 Decorate both sides of the card with patterns or pictures.

5 Fold the card along the two dotted lines as shown.

6 Stick the shells inside the folded card, one to the top, the other to the bottom.

7 To play the clappers, hold them between your thumb and index finger and click the shells together.

7.

The halves of empty coconut shells, or two yoghurt pots, can also be banged together to make clappers. Try making a slow, steady marching rhythm, a fast running sound or the clip-clop of horses' hooves.

WOOD BLOCKS

Not all percussion instruments are played by banging. You can make a very different sound by rubbing these wood blocks together.

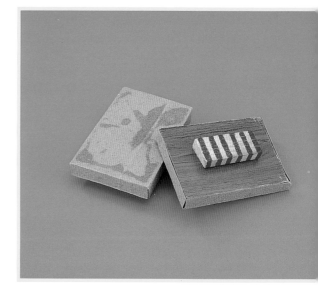

You will need:

paints or coloured paper
paste
pencil
piece of wood (about 2cm thick)
sandpaper
saw
scissors

Caution: saws can be dangerous. Ask an adult for help.

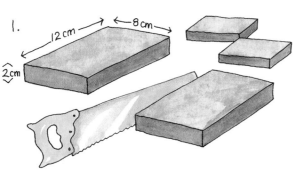

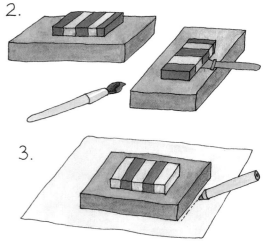

1 Saw two blocks of wood about 12cm × 8cm × 2cm.

2 To make the handles, stick a smaller block of wood to the middle of each larger one. Decorate with paints or coloured paper.

3 Lay one block on the back of a sheet of sandpaper and draw round the edge with a dotted line.

4.

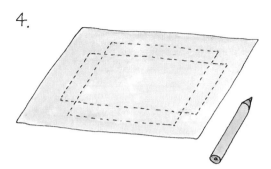

5-6.

4 Add flaps 2cm wide to the rectangle as shown.

5 Cut out and fold up the flaps. Glue the sandpaper firmly to the bottom and sides of the wood block.

6 Repeat 3, 4 and 5 with the other block.

7 Play by rubbing or banging the wood blocks together.

7.

There are many other ways of making scraping noises. Try rubbing different brushes across the following surfaces: cheese grater, egg box, corrugated card.

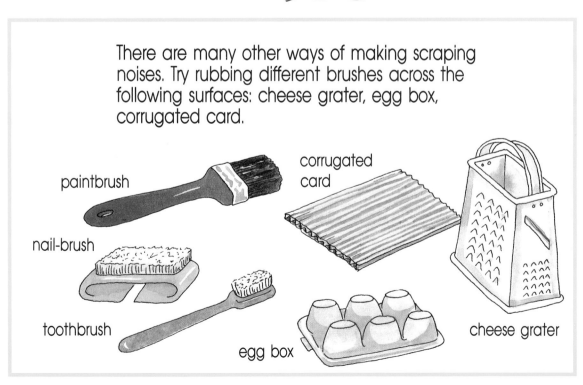

paintbrush

corrugated card

nail-brush

toothbrush

egg box

cheese grater

RHYTHM STICKS

The sharp sound of rhythm sticks make them ideal for accompanying music with a strong beat, such as West Indian calypso.

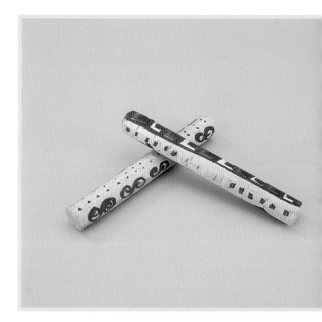

You will need:

broom handle
chisel
hammer
poster paints
sandpaper
saw

Caution: woodworking tools can be dangerous. Ask an adult for help.

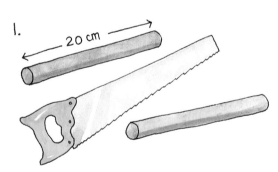

1.

20 cm

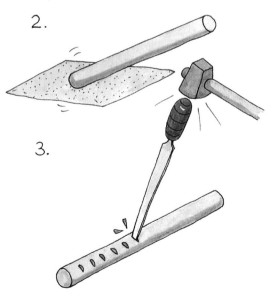

2.

3.

1 Saw two pieces of wood 20cm long from an old broom handle.

2 Smooth the ends with sandpaper.

3 Use a hammer and chisel to tap small notches in a line along one side of each stick.

4 Decorate with bright patterns using poster paints.

4.

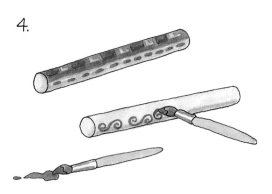

5 Play by banging the sticks together to the rhythm of the music or, to change the sound, try scraping one stick across the notched side of the other.

5.

Any number of household items can be used as drums and they all sound different. Use a variety of materials – wood, plastic, cardboard, metal. Which do you like best?

GOURD SHAKER

Many African instruments are made from hollowed-out gourds (a type of fruit). An empty plastic bottle can be used like a gourd to make a resonating sound when beads bang against it.

You will need:

fruit net
large plastic bottle
needle
scissors
selection of beads
    and buttons
strong thread

1 Cut the top fastener from the net.

2 Sew on brightly coloured beads and buttons, taking care not to sew both sides of the net together by mistake.

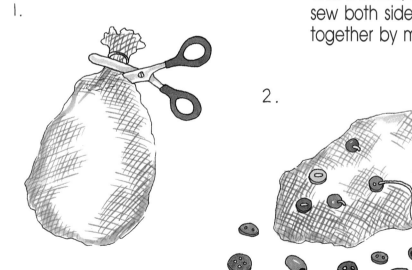

3 Turn the net inside out and place over the bottle.

4 Weave a piece of strong thread or string through the top of the net and tie round the neck of the plastic bottle.

5 Shake so that the beads bang against the bottle.

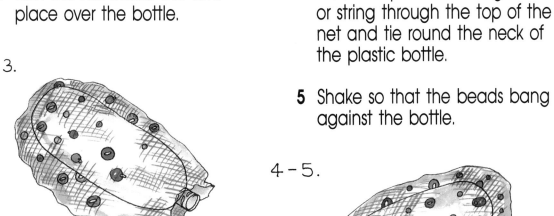

3.

4 – 5.

You can also make shakers from tins, plastic bottles or yoghurt pots covered with greaseproof paper. Fill them with split peas, lentils, small beads or gravel – each filling will produce a different sound.

split peas

gravel

lentils

beads

JAPANESE DRUM

Carry this drum in a carnival procession or use it to accompany a dance or play. As you twist the handle, the beads flick excitedly against the sound box.

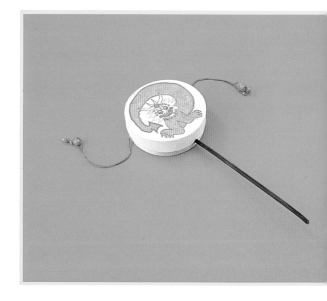

You will need:

2 beads
paints
paste
pencil
scissors
stick or garden cane
sticky tape
string
white paper
wooden cheese box

1 Place the box lid on a piece of white paper and draw round the edge.

1.

2 Cut out the circle and stick to the lid, then decorate with a colourful picture or pattern.

2.

3 Cut away a small section from the side of the box and insert the stick. Tape the stick to the base of the box as shown.

3.

4.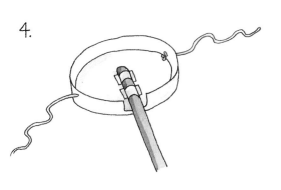

5 – 6.

4 Pierce a hole in each side of the
box. Knot two pieces of string
and thread through each hole.

5 Stick the lid firmly over the base.

6 Tie a bead on to the end of
each piece of string.

7 To play, twist the handle and
allow the beads to flick against
the box.

You can make a similar sound by cutting 1cm
× 10cm strips from a plastic bottle and taping
them to a saucepan, margarine tub or milk
bottle. Flick to produce a clicking effect.

TWEETERS

Like the bull-roarer, an ancient instrument from New Guinea, tweeters are swung wildly above the head. Safest to play outside!

You will need:

matchstick
paste
patterned paper
plastic tub with lid
scissors
sticky tape
string

1 Cut a slit 1cm wide into the side of the plastic tub and make a small hole in the bottom.

2 Cut a length of string about 30cm long.

3 Tie half a matchstick to one end of the string, then thread the other end through the hole so the stick is inside the tub.

I.

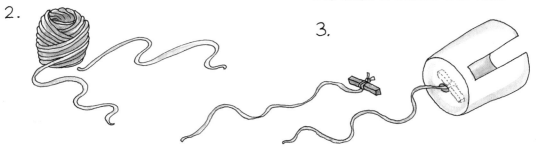

2.

3.

4.

5.

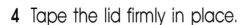

6.

4 Tape the lid firmly in place.

5 Cover with brightly patterned paper, taking care to leave the slit open.

6 Swing the tub round on the end of the string and hear it 'tweeting'.

7 Experiment using different size bottles and cartons to make different sounds.

Another way to make a note is to blow gently across the top of a glass bottle. Pour some water into the bottle and you will hear a different note. Line up several bottles, each with a different amount of water, and you will have enough notes to play a tune.

MOUTH ORGAN

The notes on this mouth organ are produced by blowing on plastic straws, causing them to vibrate, like the reed of a clarinet. You can feel your lips tingle when you play.

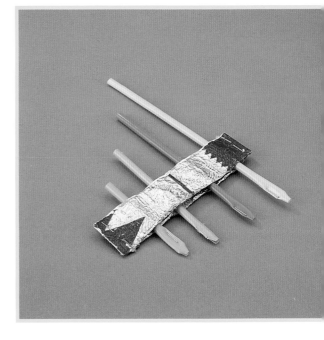

You will need:

card
paste
4 plastic drinking straws
scissors
stapler
sticky tape

1 Snip the edges from one end of a plastic drinking straw as shown.

2 Put a staple into one side of the straw just below the cut.

3 Repeat 1 and 2 for the three other straws.

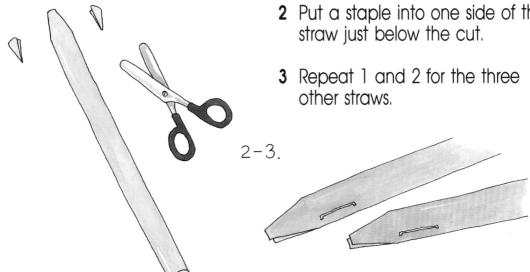

4.

4 Cut the bottom from each straw to make the following lengths: 4cm, 7cm, 11cm, 16cm.

5 Cut two strips of card, 20cm × 2cm.

5.

6 Tape the four straws along a strip of card as shown, then stick the other strip across the top.

6.

7 To play: hold each end of the card. Tighten your lips across your teeth and place the straw between your lips. Blow hard!

To make a kazoo, fold a piece of greaseproof paper across a comb. Press your lips firmly to the paper then blow air through the comb, humming a tune as you blow.

FLUTE

In many wind instruments, such as recorders and flutes, sound is produced by blowing air over a specially shaped hole.

You will need:

card
cardboard tube
greaseproof paper
paints
paste
pencil
scissors
sticky tape

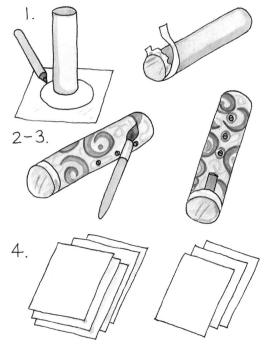

1 Cut a circle of greaseproof paper a little larger than the cardboard tube, then place over one end and tape down the edges securely.

2 Cut a rectangular hole 1.5cm × 1cm, about 1cm from the closed end of the tube. Cut three small finger-holes into the tube as shown.

3 Decorate the tube using paints or crayons.

4 To make the mouthpiece, cut five rectangles of card 2cm × 3.5cm, and three rectangles of the same size from greaseproof paper.

5.

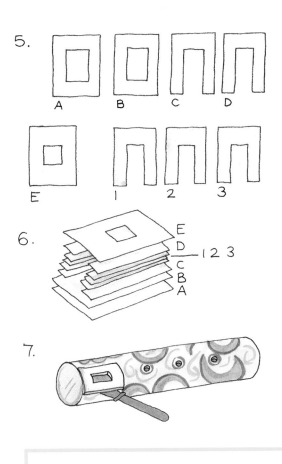

5 Cut windows 1cm × 1.5cm in cards A and B.
Cut doors 1cm × 2.5cm in cards C and D.
Cut a window 1cm square in the middle of card E.
Cut doors 1cm × 2cm in the three pieces of paper.

6.

6 Stick B on to A, and C on top of B. Then stick the three pieces of greaseproof paper on to C. Finally, stick D to the paper, and E on top of D. Leave to dry.

7.

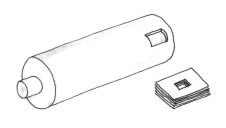

7 Stick the mouthpiece over the hole at the top of your flute as shown. Blow gently to produce a note.

Use the same mouthpiece design to make a hoo-hoo.

Cut a rectangular hole, 1.5cm × 1cm, 1cm from the bottom of a plastic bottle. Stick the mouthpiece over the hole.

To play the hoo-hoo, move your finger in and out of the neck of the bottle as you blow.

ZITHER

Zithers are a favourite with musicians in many parts of the world. You can make a zither using a flat board. Place it in a shoe-box and you will increase the sound.

You will need:

cardboard shoe-box	pencil
6 elastic bands	saw
hammer	scissors
12 nails	sticky tape
paints	wooden
paste	board

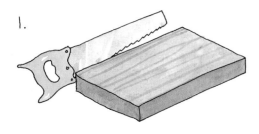
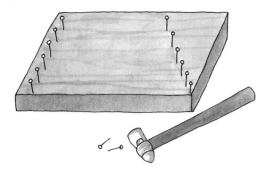

Caution: woodworking tools can be dangerous. Ask an adult for help.

1 Cut a wooden board to fit tightly into the top of a cardboard shoe-box.

2 Using a pencil, make six evenly spaced marks along one of the short sides of the wood. Hammer a nail a little way into each mark.

3 Draw a diagonal line from one of the opposite corners as shown, then hammer the other six nails along the line.

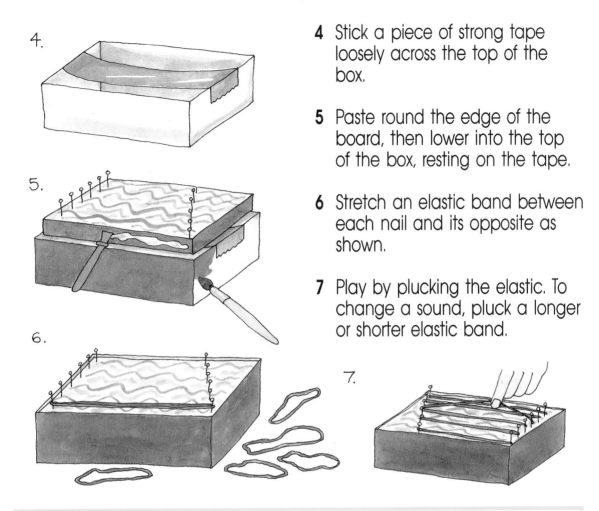

4 Stick a piece of strong tape loosely across the top of the box.

5 Paste round the edge of the board, then lower into the top of the box, resting on the tape.

6 Stretch an elastic band between each nail and its opposite as shown.

7 Play by plucking the elastic. To change a sound, pluck a longer or shorter elastic band.

Write music for your zither.

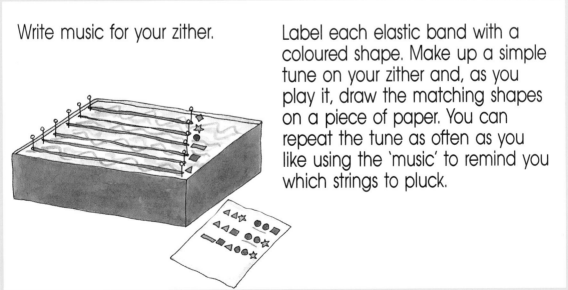

Label each elastic band with a coloured shape. Make up a simple tune on your zither and, as you play it, draw the matching shapes on a piece of paper. You can repeat the tune as often as you like using the 'music' to remind you which strings to pluck.

SARANGI

This one-stringed instrument comes from India. It can be plucked like a guitar, or played with a bow like a cello.

You will need:

cork	piece of wood
drill	(3cm × 50cm
fishing line (1m)	× 1cm)
greaseproof paper	poster paints
margarine tub	scissors
paste	tissue paper
pencil	

Caution: woodworking tools can be dangerous. Ask an adult for help.

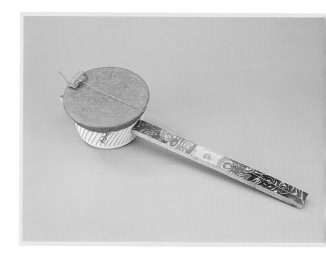

1 Trace round the top of an empty margarine tub on to a piece of greaseproof paper. Draw another circle about 2cm bigger round the outside.

2 Cut round the larger circle, then use as a template to cut three more greaseproof paper circles and four tissue paper circles.

3 Firmly stick one of the greaseproof circles over the top of the plastic tub, then paste on a tissue circle, pulling it gently to avoid wrinkles. Leave to dry.

4 Repeat 3 until you have used all the paper, making sure that each layer is pulled tightly across the tub and dry before adding the next.

5 Cut slits either side of the tub, big enough for the wood to fit through.

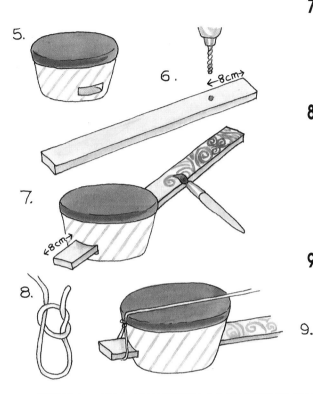

6 Bore a hole at a spot 8cm from one end of the piece of wood.

7 Push the other end through the tub until about 8cm juts out of the other side. Decorate with paints.

8 Tie a slip knot in the fishing line as shown. Hook the loop over the short end of the wood, then pull tightly over the tub and tie through the hole at the other end.

9 Cut the cork in half and stick under the string as a bridge.

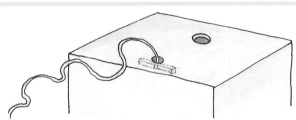

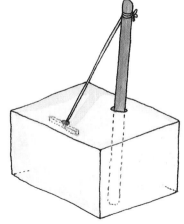

To make a double bass. Tie a small stick to the end of a piece of string, then thread the other end through the top of a cardboard box so that the stick is held inside. Make a larger hole in the top of the box and push a broom handle through it. Tie the string to the top of the broom handle, then pluck the string to make a sound.

BOOK LIST

If you want some more ideas for making musical instruments then these books may be of interest. Your local library should be able to get copies for you.

Deshpande, Chris.
SCRAPE, RATTLE AND BLOW
A & C Black, 1988.   *0713629886*
The story of one class of school children and how they made musical instruments from various junk items.

R. Thompson.
MY CLASS MAKES MUSIC
Franklin Watts, 1986.   *0863134459*
A class of children seen preparing and performing some music and dance for the school assembly. They used a mixture of instruments they made themselves, together with a cello, a guitar, a xylophone and others from the school.

Perkins, Ginny.
DISCOVER MAKING MUSIC
Simon & Schuster, 1990.   *0750000074*
Four children buy a coconut and we watch them turning it into a pair of maracas.

For older children

McLean, Margaret.
MAKING MUSICAL INSTRUMENTS
MacMillan, 1982.   *0333308573*
Further ideas for making music, which use a wider range of materials and instruments. A few simple tunes to try are included at the end of the book.

Willson, Robina Beckles.
MUSIC MAKER
Viking Kestrel, 1986.   *0670805270*
More detailed ideas for making things like one string guitars and rubber trumpets. Shows how to create and note tunes and gives ideas for pieces to perform and sound games to play.

INDEX